Sea Urchins

Simon Rose

www.av2books.com

AV² provides enriched content that supplements and complements this book. Weigl's AV² books strive to create inspired learning and engage young minds in a total learning experience.

Go to **www.av2books.com**, and enter this book's unique code.

Your AV² Media Enhanced books come alive with...

Audio
Listen to sections of the book read aloud.

Key Words
Study vocabulary, and complete a matching word activity.

Video
Watch informative video clips.

Quizzes
Test your knowledge.

BOOK CODE

L28751

Embedded Weblinks
Gain additional information for research.

Slide Show
View images and captions, and prepare a presentation.

AV² by Weigl brings you media enhanced books that support active learning.

Try This!
Complete activities and hands-on experiments.

... and much, much more!

Published by AV² by Weigl
350 5th Avenue, 59th Floor New York, NY 10118
Website: www.av2books.com   www.weigl.com

Library of Congress Cataloging-in-Publication Data

Rose, Simon, 1961-
 Sea urchins / Simon Rose.
   p. cm. -- (Ocean life)
 Includes index.
 ISBN 978-1-61690-691-7 (hardcover : alk. paper) -- ISBN 978-1-61690-695-5 (softcover : alk. paper)
 1. Sea urchins--Juvenile literature. I. Title.
 QL384.E2R67 2012
 593.9'5--dc22

                    2010050418

Printed in the United States of America in North Mankato, Minnesota
1 2 3 4 5 6 7 8 9 0   15 14 13 12 11

052011
WEP37500

Project Coordinator: Aaron Carr
Art Director: Terry Paulhus

Weigl acknowledges Getty Images, Dreamstime, iStockphoto, and Peter Arnold as image suppliers for this title.

CONTENTS

What is a Sea Urchin?

Have you ever seen a fish that looks like a cactus? It may have been a sea urchin. Sea urchins are small, round, and covered with long **spines** that can move.

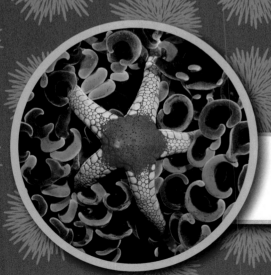

Sea urchins are in the same family as starfish.

5

Sea Urchin Size

Have you ever played baseball? Sea urchins are about the same size as a baseball. They are usually about 2 to 4 inches (5 to 10 centimeters) wide. The largest sea urchin in the world is the red sea urchin. It is about 7.5 inches (19 cm) wide.

Red sea urchins are one of the longest living animals on Earth. They live as long as 200 years.

Under the Sea

Have you ever swam in the ocean? Sea urchins can be found in all of Earth's oceans. Most sea urchins live on the ocean floor near rocky shorelines. They can also be found in rock pools, kelp forests, and on **coral**. Sea urchins live in water that can be as deep as 15,000 feet (4,572 meters).

9

Body Armor

Have you ever worn hard padding to play a sport? Sea urchins have a hard shell. This shell is covered with sharp spines. The spines are about 2 to 4 inches (5 to 10 cm) long. They stick out like small spears in every direction but down. Many sea urchins have **venom** in their spines. The venom protects sea urchins from **predators**.

Moving Around

How does a ball covered in spines move around? Sea urchins use their spines to crawl across the ocean floor. They also have tube feet that are **hollow** and strong. Each tube has a sucker on the end. Sea urchins can stick these suckers onto objects. They can use their spines and tube feet to pull themselves in any direction.

The long-spined black sea urchin has spines that can be up to 12 inches (30 cm) long.

Hiding Places

How can brightly colored sea urchins hide from predators? Sea urchins use their tube feet to pick up seaweed, small rocks, or pieces of shells. Then, they place these objects over their body. This helps sea urchins match the area around them.

Crabs, eels, and large fish all hunt sea urchins for food.

Urchin Eats

Can you imagine having a mouth on your feet? A sea urchin's mouth is on the underside of its body. The mouth looks like a claw. It is surrounded by five teeth that look like plates. Sea urchins eat food off the ground as they move.

The sea urchin's favorite foods are seaweed, small pieces of animals, and **algae**. Sea urchins scrape their food from rocks and the ocean floor.

17

Seafood

Did you know some people eat sea urchins? Sea urchins are a popular food in much of Asia. They are most popular in Japan. More than 80 percent of all sea urchins caught are sent to Japan. Red, green, and purple sea urchins are sold as food most often.

Sea urchins are a favorite food of the California sea otter.

19

Saving Sea Urchins

Why are there fewer sea urchins this year than last? Sea urchins are affected by **pollution**. Oil and **chemicals** that spill into the ocean can harm sea urchins. Even noise can be harmful. Sea urchins use their sense of touch to move around and find food. Large boats and drills make so much noise that the ground shakes. Sea urchins cannot find food or places to hide.

Sea urchins are also at risk from fishing. People take too many to eat.

Make Your Own Sea Urchin

Supplies
colored toothpicks, modeling clay, paint

1. Roll the modeling clay into a ball. The ball can be as big or small as you like.

2. Choose at least 15 toothpicks to make your sea urchin. Big sea urchins will need many spines. Pick as many toothpick colors as you can to make your sea urchin.

3. Stick the toothpicks into the clay ball. The toothpicks should cover your sea urchin.

4. When you have finished sticking in all of the spines, leave your sea urchin to dry for three hours.

Glossary

algae: green, slimy plants that grow in the ocean

chemicals: man-made substances

coral: a hard object in the ocean that is made by a small sea animal

hollow: empty inside

pollution: harmful substances put into water

predators: animals that hunt other animals for food

spines: thin, hard, pointy parts of the body

venom: a liquid poison animals use to protect themselves

Index

Log on to www.av2books.com

AV² by Weigl brings you media enhanced books that support active learning. Go to www.av2books.com, and enter the special code found on page 2 of this book. You will gain access to enriched and enhanced content that supplements and complements this book. Content includes video, audio, web links, quizzes, a slide show, and activities.

Audio
Listen to sections of
the book read aloud.

Video
Watch informative video clips.

Embedded Weblinks
Gain additional information
for research.

Try This!
Complete activities and
hands-on experiments.

WHAT'S ONLINE?

 Try This!

Gain a better understanding of a sea urchin's size with a fun comparison activity.

Identify the benefits of sea urchins' defensive adaptations.

Complete a fun coloring activity.

 Embedded Weblinks

Find more information about sea urchins.

Check out myths and legends about sea urchins.

More on sea urchins' diets and nutrition.

 Video

Watch an introductory video to sea urchins.

Watch a video of a sea urchin in its natural environment.

EXTRA FEATURES

Audio
Listen to sections of the book read aloud.

Key Words
Study vocabulary, and complete a matching word activity.

Slide Show
View images and captions, and prepare a presentation.

Quizzes
Test your knowledge.

AV² was built to bridge the gap between print and digital. We encourage you to tell us what you like and what you want to see in the future. Sign up to be an AV² Ambassador at www.av2books.com/ambassador.